Joe Girard, best selling author and motivational speaker—one of Larry's primary and principal mentors—writes:

> Larry Krakow speaks from experience—lots of it—and that is the key. *Winning Salesmanship— The Glengarry Way* offers compelling, candid, cutting edge lessons—with specific closing techniques—to increase your income and success.

—Joe Girard
World's Greatest Salesperson
Author of *How to Sell Anything to Anybody*
www.joegirard.com

Steve Chandler, best selling author, master coach and speaker—a significant source of inspiration, motivation, and support for Larry—writes:

> "Finally! A book about sales that doesn't pussyfoot around! This book smacks you between the eyes and leaves you ready to rock the world!"

—Steve Chandler
Author of *The Joy of Selling*
www.stevechandler.com

Winning Salesmanship — The Glengarry Way

Larry Krakow

Robert D. Reed Publishers • Bandon, OR

Copyright © 2009 by Larry Krakow

All rights reserved.

Robert D. Reed Publishers
P.O. Box 1992
Bandon, OR 97411
Phone: 541-347-9882 • Fax: -9883
E-mail: 4bobreed@msn.com
web site: www.rdrpublishers.com

Cover Designer: **Cleone L. Reed**
Editor: **Kate Rakini**
Interior Designer: **Barbara Kruger**

ISBN 978-1-934759-27-1
        1-934759-27-9

Library of Congress Control Number 2008943535

Manufactured, typeset and printed in the United States of America

Mixed Sources
Product group from well-managed forests and other controlled sources
www.fsc.org Cert no. SW-COC-002283
© 1996 Forest Stewardship Council

Acknowledgments

First, I want to thank my family—Penny, Jonny, Becca, and Sam Krakow, Robert Krakow, Barry and Jessica Krakow, and Bette Weigert; I cherish them, their love, and their involvement in my life. Robert, I thank you for always being here for us, especially for Jonny and me. I want to express deepest gratitude and love to my parents who taught me to live with integrity, strength, and compassion—my mother, Marion, whose gentle wisdom, humor, and loving support has been a constant inspiration to me throughout the years, and my father, Bernard, of blessed memory, who was an exceptional role model and consistent source of love and encouragement. I miss him very much.

I am also grateful to have Bernice and Eddie Cohen, and Wendy and Oren Penn in my life; they are very special and important to me. Tot Filderman, thank you for giving me my first sales job. Lynne Filderman, thank you for your valuable input and assistance. I wish to acknowledge my entire family for the many ways they have affected my life.

Rabbi Sholom B. Korf has been an invaluable source of friendship and guidance; I am very grateful for his kind assistance and profound insights. Rabbi Meir Kessler has also influenced my life on several levels and I am thankful for his support. I appreciate the caring dedication of Roberto Cohen. Thank you, Alon Cohen for being a great help to me. I thank Kathy Goldstein for helping me with this project from start to finish.

Special thanks are extended to Nicole Bourassa, Jerry and Lisa Reid, Linda and Omar Baez, Frank and Phyllis Aliberti, Ed and

Anne McClosky, Mr. Abe Miller, and Mr. Mac Page for their friendship and support.

Joe Girard, thank you for being one of my first and most powerful mentors. Stephen Chandler, thank you for your consideration, help, and motivation. Robert Reed and staff, thank you for your efforts and alliance. David Mamet, thank you for writing such an effective, significant, and powerful portrayal of salesmen and selling. Many people have helped me throughout my life on both a professional and personnel level. I am grateful to all who have given me support.

Most of all, I thank God for all of my many blessings—the people, love, successes, and learning experiences of my life. May I live the type of life He wants me to lead.

Contents

Introduction

I wrote this book to help you close sales—lots of them—and to close hard. By hard closing I mean persistent, careful, pre-planned closing. Whether you are a beginner, intermediate, or advanced salesperson, I will help you close more sales and increase your income with confidence and skill.

It will be useful for you to be familiar with the 1992 film *Glengarry Glen Ross* written by David Mamet. You can Google *YouTube*[2] *Glengarry Glen Ross Alec Baldwin*, or buy or rent the video. Based on Mamet's award-winning play about four desperate real estate agents, believe me, this scenario happened all the time in car dealerships, insurance agencies, and probably life insurance and real estate firms, too.

Watch the beginning scene where Alec Baldwin, as Blake, the manager, leads a sales meeting; this is the most important part of the movie. It's a little harsh. You don't necessarily have to watch the entire *Glengarry Glen Ross*; I will give you a lot of sales tips whether you view it or not.

We are going to explore the basic concepts of closing—getting your clients to agree to the sale. I want to make it very clear that you will learn essential closing techniques—how to close and close hard with integrity—because to me, that is really what successful selling is all about.

You can buy all of the different sales books, and we can talk about contacts, networking, and how to get in front of people. But if you don't have what I consider to be the number one ability—closing the deal, or as Baldwin says in *Glengarry Glen Ross*, getting them to sign on the line that is dotted—you probably won't get the sale.

We are going to have a great time going through this book. I have many, many years of salesmanship. I was on the front lines. I spent years in the car dealership. Later, I became one of the top producing insurance agents in the country. Over the years, I've also trained hundreds of agents. I know how to get inside people's heads, and how to sell, how to close, and how to do it the right way.

I am going to give you a lot of insight into how to close and how to close the proper way—not in a pushy, obnoxious way. I will teach you my concepts for effectively closing the deal with grace and candor.

I would like you to sit back and relax. This is a very short read; complete the entire book and highlight areas of interest. Do as I say, exactly as I say, and you will find an increase in your sales. Don't deviate from my knowledge; use my lines word for word—they work. My words and techniques will help you close your clients and improve your earnings.

If you read my book and say, "I am going to just take a little piece of this or a part of that," and then it doesn't' work for you, that's why. You must use my closing techniques word for word. And, do you know what? I gladly make this guarantee to you: if your closing ability does not improve, send my book back for a full refund.

So get ready. This book is going to make you laugh when I share my anecdotes in the sales business; it might even give you some goose bumps. Just sit back. Grab a cup of coffee, if you'd like, and let's get started. To reiterate, highlight areas you will benefit from, and learn my closing techniques word for word so that, as Baldwin says in *Glengarry Glen Ross*, you will "ABC— Always Be Closing."

Good luck! I will see you on the other side of *Winning Salesmanship—The Glengarry Way*.

Chapter 1

Put That Coffee Down—Coffee Is for Closers!

This is exactly what we are going to be talking about—closing. I am going to give you what I believe are some of the main components of closing a sale.

Let's go back to the title of this chapter—*Put That Coffee Down—Coffee Is for Closers!* This is probably the most famous line of David Mamet's 1992 film, *Glengarry Glen Ross*. As Levine, the *schlumpy* (Yiddish for sloppy or dowdy) salesman played by Jack Lemmon, was getting up for a cup of coffee during a meeting, Alec Baldwin orders him to "Put that coffee down—coffee is for closers!"

When you are in a situation where you are going to close, you have to close hard. When you are a salesman, whether you are selling cars, insurance, retail, any tangible or intangible product, your main job is to get that person to sign on the dotted line, agree to take delivery, or agree to go with the contract—and to do it with integrity.

Your main goal, of course, is getting that person to say "Yes!" And herein lies the key. So many salesmen are very good talkers and very good *schmoozers*,[3] but they find it very difficult to get the person to say "Yes!" It's been my experience during many years of closing and salesmanship that very few people have ever looked at me and said, "Yes, I'll take it." It's usually much more subtle than that, and that is one of the main topics I want to talk about in this chapter.

Close right from the beginning, very, very hard, and then establish rapport after closing.

The first part is the "meet and greet." You may find this odd, but I'm not a big *schmoozer*. I don't concentrate on building rapport in the beginning. I'm straightforward; I'm there to do business. I'm not there to waste my time or my client's time. When you go to a doctor's office and the doctor comes in to see you, you don't want to hear 30-40 minutes of "Where did your kids grow up? Where's your family? Where did you go to school?" A good doctor knows this. He comes in and asks, "How are you? Where are you from? It's nice to meet you." Right after this, he quickly gets down to business and asks, "What's wrong? What is the problem?"

If you are a good salesman and you want to get better, you want to go in with confidence whether your customers are coming to you or you are greeting them. And you want to start getting down to business quickly. I'll tell you why and how it works to build rapport after, and not before, you close.

When I enter a home to sell financial or insurance products, I normally spend only a few minutes of "How are you doing?" and "Where are you from?" with my clients. After this I stress the reason I'm there in the first place. I'm there to close and help them with their situation. As Zig Ziglar, leading sales motivator, and other successful sales professionals say, "You help get them what they want, so that you get what you want."

My point here is this: I'll close, right from the beginning, very, very hard, and then I will establish rapport after closing. I may see clients to write a very, very big financial case, perhaps a life insurance policy or an annuity product. Once I've gotten them to agree to go to the paperwork and start signing, I will put everything aside at that point to begin my rapport-building and *schmoozing*.

We will talk about objections and various closes throughout the book. But the first point I want to stress is to go in with a matter of fact "How are you doing? Let's get down to business." As I am closing, and I am always closing, I'm there in a matter of fact way. I'm talking, getting down to business.

Thirty minutes into the presentation, when I've already sold my clients and gotten them "to sign on the line," then, of course, I'll sit with them 20 or 30 minutes and ask, "Where do your kids live? Where are you from? What kind of work do you do?" I'll get them past what I call some initial buyer's remorse[4] as I build rapport.

Your time is important.
Remember that.
You're going in to close.
You're going in to help
    provide a service to your clients.
You're going in to make money.

The next morning, no matter how small or large the case, I always call my clients to say I need additional signatures, or to let them know I just checked with "So-and-So" and everything is going well. This will preempt any further buyer's remorse right then and there.

When you are a good salesman, your aim is to do business and that's it. You establish a little rapport, what is called "common ground," and then you close—close hard—and close in a nice, subtle way so that your clients do not feel threatened. This will work for you. These techniques will work for you.

Also keep in mind that you must have a thorough knowledge about what you are selling. When I was in sales in various businesses or industries, you could throw everything at me as an objection to a particular product—including the kitchen sink—and I knew the item and how to respond.

When I was in the financial sector selling life insurance, I would read and read and read, voraciously, until two, three, or four in the morning, to learn about the product. When I worked my way up in various businesses to become sales manager, I knew the product backwards and forwards. When people came into my office, I knew my product—this is very important. Show me a top-notch salesperson, a tremendous closer, and I'll also show you someone who knows his product.

There's also an old saying, "Know your customers." Get inside their heads. Learn about the type of people who buy your particular product so that you know your customers. When a client gives me an objection, I know in which direction to go because I know I've dealt with these types of people. Always study. Always learn. Everyone will tell you this. "Pick up other sales books. Pick up motivational books."

I've been in the sales industry for over 20 years and, believe me, I've read all of the motivational books and all of the books by accomplished salesmen—Joe Girard, Tom Hopkins, Zig Ziglar, and others. They all offer excellent sales techniques. Today, you have to say, "Look—I have to close hard."

I'm not telling you, as they used to say, you have to stand on the person until they give you a check, because he or she will turn around and cancel on you the next day anyway. I am talking about closing, closing, closing on that particular product.

Your time is valuable, too. If I am with clients, I'm there to help them. But, if after a certain point I see that I can't really help them, I leave.

A salesman recently came to me and said, "I don't believe it. I went in. We spoke for 30-40 minutes. I had the best rapport. His son apparently went to the same school that I did—the same university. It was unbelievable. Then I got down to the product, and what did they say? 'Oh, we want to think about it.'"

Forget it. Your time is important. Remember that. You're going in to close. You're going in to help provide a service to your clients. You're going in to make money. Yes, you're going to help them, but you're going in there to earn money and to make a living.

If a person is going to jerk you around, get up and go, because you're not going to make any money in there and your time is precious. Watch out for that. People don't care. People are looking at you as a salesman; they don't care that you've got a family to feed. They'll waste your time longer than anyone else out there. Get in and get out.

You must also believe in the product. You will often hear stories about this, and I really don't want to spend time talking about how you have to love your product, it's an extension of you, that they're buying you, etc. The bottom line is, yes—it's true. You have to stand behind your product and believe in it, or you will have a lot of trouble out there and be considered a shyster.

My book is for the person who says, "I like my job. I love my product. I like the service I provide, but I need to close another 20%–30%. I need to be able to close more because I'm already getting in front of a lot of people, but I'm only closing 10%–20%. I need to get that figure to 20%–30%." Of course you need to get it to that—that means more money for you. And that's what I'm trying to show you here—how to increase your income. All I care about is getting you to close more successfully. Soak it up.

Chapter 2

You Call Yourself a Salesman, You Son of a Bitch!

So many sales people out there don't look the part. I'm going to start with the subject of grooming and end with the importance of trying to close a sale regardless of whether a customer dresses up or dresses down.

For you advanced salespeople who know how to dress, you can skip this part. I'm keeping it very short. But many salespeople are hurting themselves by the way they dress and by the way they carry themselves. So I want to take a look at this. Again, we're going into closing, but be set up to close. This is important.

I know you've heard it before. I know you've read it in "Dress for Success" books, but it really needs to be said again. I'll quote David J. Schwartz, Ph. D. in *The Magic of Thinking Big*[5]: "Rather than buying three or four nice suits, buy one or two expensive suits, and then just use them."

I remember when I first started out presenting seminars. I had one very expensive Giorgio Armani suit that I wore to my seminars. I wore Ferragamo shoes, a Ferragamo belt, a Neiman Marcus shirt, and a Versace tie with a top of the line suit. As soon as I finished with my seminar, I went home, hung it in the closet, and then wore it for the next seminar.

When you are in front of people, especially at a seminar, and you are doing business with seminars, by all means, you must have a top of the line wardrobe. If you are seeing people on a daily basis,

**Look good and look successful—
    they're looking at you.
Believe me, those first impressions matter.**

then go and get yourself two suits and a nice watch, shoes, and belt. Spend—because you want to look that part.

I'm not saying that you have to look intimidating; it depends upon the line you're in. Some people like to look casual. They might be selling to people whose required dress is a knit company shirt.

I'm talking about a situation in which you have to close and have to close hard—for example, real estate sales, insurance sales, sales in a car dealership. Look good and look successful—they're looking at you. Believe me, those first impressions matter.

Hair grooming, hygiene—everything counts. I happen to keep my hair very short. I also don't have a lot of hair, but I keep it short. I get a trim once a week and shave daily. Keep your nails clean and short. Nasal hair must never be noticeable. Make sure your ears are clean. Be meticulous about dental hygiene. Brush your teeth often and make sure you always have fresh breath. Always wear clean, pressed clothing. Your shoes must shine. So many good salesmen ignore their appearance and it hurts them.

Many books are written about motivation, the magic of thinking big, and thinking positive. You do have to think big and think positive. These principles are all great, but you also have to look the part. Act as *if*.

Don't be looked upon as a "*schlumpy* salesperson." Look successful. If you have to go out and buy a few things on a credit card—a nice watch, for example—do it. You can pick up a Movado watch reasonably, or look for sales. I personally wear a Breitling. It's a fine watch, and I prefer the large dial and bezel of the Breitling, but you don't have to go that far. You don't have to jump into Rolex just yet; just look the part.

There is one other thing I want to stress about dress. Most *schlumpy* salespeople will let a customer walk on by if they aren't dressed well. I made one of the biggest sales of my career from a guy nobody else wanted to look at—a guy who looked as if he came off an immigrant truck from Laredo, Texas. He turned out to be one of my biggest sales because nobody bothered to take the time with him.

Julia Roberts, as Vivian Ward in J. F. Lawton's 1990 film *Pretty Woman*, is a great example of this. When she's dressed like a

**Treat everybody like they're gold—
like they're Donald Trump.
I don't care how they're dressed
or how they look.
It is the right thing to do and
it will reap dividends.**

hooker and tries to shop in a high-end store by herself, she is snubbed and humiliated by the salesperson who believes she will gain nothing from her. With Richard Gere, as Edward Lewis, the wealthy businessman, at her side, the salespeople and sales manager cannot do enough to satisfy both of them as they shop.

Even more important, do you remember the snobby salesperson who wouldn't give Roberts a chance? Her astonished face, when Roberts returns to the store dressed as a chic lady loaded with packages, carried the pain of her loss of all current and future commissions from Roberts.

Try it. Get all dressed up in your nicest suit and walk into Bloomingdales, Nordstrom's, or Macy's. Go into the men's department and see how quickly the salespeople surround you. Go in again the next day wearing a tee shirt, a pair of jeans, and tennis shoes. No one will give you the time of day. That's because most *schlep*[6] salespeople, especially in retail, have no idea that a lot of guys with money will purposely go dressed down to look around in a store and not be harassed.

Do yourself a favor. Greet everyone as if they're a Donald Trump. You're going to be there for them and service them even though you have no idea what you're doing with that person, or what they're like.

One time I went into a home with an insurance product and the people really didn't have a lot of money. I spent a good amount of time helping them out with some Medicare issues. I made some phone calls and made sure they had some claims covered. As I was walking out the door, knowing I had no sale, they said, "By the way, we have a relative down the road and we're going to get you in there because he has a couple of policies." And I went in and sold him a big policy—a very big policy. It made my week.

You never know where the sale is going to come from. Dress and act your part. Treat everybody like they're gold—like they're Donald Trump. I don't care how they're dressed or how they look. It is the right thing to do and it will reap dividends.

I don't care what level you're at.
You may have been the greatest
   salesman in real estate, and
   now you're in insurance, or
   vice versa.
You must seek out the top people
   for advice, and you must choose
   your words carefully.

Chapter 3

The Good News Is, "You're Fired!"

In the movie *Glengarry Glen Ross*, Alec Baldwin makes a joke that, "The good news is you're fired, and you have all but another week to get some sales to redeem yourselves. "

I think this is very true in sales. Sometimes, you have to really go with your back against the wall and believe this is your last week or you will lose your position. Sometimes, that's what it takes.

When I was a sales manager, I used to tell salesmen, "You have a week to keep your job." As a sales manager in the car business helping my salespeople close a customer, I literally said to them, "You'd better go back and tell the customer this word for word or you're going to lose your job." At times that was the only thing I could do to light a fire under that salesperson. Sometimes you really have to be pressed. You have to be almost at your wit's end, and then it will turn for you.

I knew how to close. When I would tell an agent or a salesperson who reported to me to say something word for word, I meant it. I'm going to say it again and again throughout this book— learn my techniques for closing word for word.

Here is an example of how the right words made the difference. When I first started in the insurance business, I lived in Clearwater, FL, and was given the territory of West Palm Beach. I traveled down there, stayed in a hotel, and physically knocked on doors holding letters from people who had requested information.

"Check your ego at the door."

If you go into a sales meeting thinking you're "Mr. Big" from another company and you need to ask certain things of someone, check your ego at the door.

It isn't a question of swallowing your pride—this is your livelihood.

I did this for two or three weeks and could not believe it—I did not make one sale. Recently married, I drove home on the weekends and said to my wife, "I can't believe this. I was a top salesman in the car business. I've always been good in sales. I can't sell one insurance product to a retiree."

When I knocked on someone's door, I said, "Hi, you mailed in this information. Can we speak? Can we get together?" And the door slammed.

The company had sales meetings in St. Petersburg, FL, which I attended. They brought in lunch and then introduced the top sales people for the week. The owner told some great motivational stories which, believe it or not, inspired me. Previously I was one of the guys who said, "Let me sell. Leave me alone." But I attended those meetings and was surprised how, even though I felt I was a successful sales person, I always picked up something new.

Anyway, as I said, after knocking on doors for three weeks, I was 0 for 50; I really, really struck out! I began talking to a salesman who had been at the company for quite awhile. He was fairly successful and I asked him, "What is the key?"

"The key is you've got to get in the door. Once you get in the door, you will find that most people, most retirees, are interested in what you have, and if you have a good product," he said.

After that conversation, I changed four words of my presentation at the door. Remember, I was holding an envelope with information that they mailed to our firm; I was not calling them cold. I knocked on their door and, when they answered, said, "Hi, you mailed a request for some information. May I step in?" "May I step in"—those four words changed everything. And they changed my life in the insurance business because the people always said, "Sure."

I went in, sat at their kitchen table, and showed them the products we had. At the time, we really did have good products—senior citizen products. After that week, I instantly became one of the top salesmen.

And this goes back to exactly what I've been saying. I was at my wit's end. I really believe that if I had another week of blanking—another week of zero—I don't think I could have made it.

Have a positive attitude and be a positive
   thinker.
What is the famous Chinese saying?
"He who does not have a smile on his face
   should not own a shop."

When the salesman gave me this advice, I sucked it up. I don't care what level you're at. You may have been the greatest salesman in real estate, and now you're in insurance, or vice versa. You must seek out the top people for advice, and you must choose your words carefully.

There is a famous saying that I often mention at sales meetings and in life: "Check your ego at the door." If you go into a sales meeting thinking you're "Mr. Big" from another company and you need to ask certain things of someone, check your ego at the door. It isn't a question of swallowing your pride—this is your livelihood.

If you meet salesmen, soak up everything you can. Read various books. Go to sales seminars. Learn how to listen and soak up everything you can about closing and selling to achieve success. Take in methods from other salespeople. You can always learn a new technique. Have a positive attitude and be a positive thinker. What is the famous Chinese saying? "He who does not have a smile on his face should not own a shop."

I really thought I was a top-notch closer. When I entered the insurance business, though, some of my mentors taught me phenomenal closes. Remember, you can touch and see a car. When you're selling an intangible product as a stock broker or insurance person, you can't touch it. You must make a transition to help your clients understand the product without showing it to them. It's not like the car business, selling a boat, or real estate. It can be difficult, but if you hang with it, you will be victorious. And I'm showing you methods throughout this book to sell and close either of them—a tangible or intangible product. You will succeed.

**I've come across probably 500-1,000
sales people in my history, and
only a very small percentage could
actually close a deal.
Many people have product knowledge
and good speaking and
communication skills.
They're people persons, but
they cannot close the deal.**

Chapter 4

Have I Got Your Attention Now?

Sales books are a dime a dozen. What I am strictly concentrating on with you in these pages is hard-core closing. When I talk about closing, I like to say that closing is everything. But it must be said, I am under the assumption that you, the person reading this book, are a person of integrity. You do the right thing for your clients. I'm not out with all my tough talk to just close people, no matter what, to make the sale. I don't believe in that at all. I do, however, want to stress that closing, "ABC—Always Be Closing," as mentioned in *Glengarry Glen Ross*, is the true course of a genuine salesman.

Many publications are written about follow-up and customer service. Again, this book does not focus on these topics. As I said, I'm going to assume that you will do the right thing for your client—that once you make the sale, you will follow up, take care of that person, and seek to get referrals. I am not going to delve into how to get more referrals and bring in more business. This is a hard-core closures book that offers lessons to help you close more deals with finesse and conviction.

I've read virtually every sales book, especially when I was in the car business years ago. You can even pick up books about various closing techniques, such as the Ben Franklin Close.[7] Again, what I am trying to do is just strictly present ideas for closing, and closing hard.

This chapter asks, "Have I Got Your Attention Now?" Well, I hope I have your attention because from here on out, you are going

If you have that one missing link—
I don't care how good you are with people,
    how attractive you are,
    how great your hygiene is,
    how great your hair is combed,
    and how nice your suit is—forget it.
You must be able to close.

to learn to close, and close the deal hard—whether you are in insurance, the car business, real estate, or computer sales. I don't care what type of sales you're in. You'd better learn this magic of closing.

Many people I interview talk a great game and say, "I need marketing—just get me in front of people," but are no good at closing. There are very, very few people who are top closers in this industry.

I went through a period of time as a sales manager in the insurance business where I must have hired hundreds of agents—and very few of them could close. I've come across probably 500-1,000 sales people in my history, and only a very small percentage could actually close a deal. Many people have product knowledge and good speaking and communication skills. They're people persons, but they cannot close the deal.

If you have that one missing link—I don't care how good you are with people, how attractive you are, how great your hygiene is, how great your hair is combed, and how nice your suits is—forget it. You must be able to close. Listen what I have to say here and get it down verbatim. This is exactly what you have to do. Now, let's really get into the meat of it.

Many of us can make excuses that
   "the leads are weak, we don't
   have customers, the customers
   we have are tire kickers and lot
   lizards—they're not looking to buy."
But I want you to turn that around
   and understand something.
When I first started out, even when
   I had a customer who was not
   a buyer and was just a shopper,
   I still would try 5, 6, 7, 8, or 9
   closing techniques on that person
   just to gain the experience.

Chapter 5

The Leads Are Weak? You're Weak!

Now we are going to get into the specifics of closing. And, as the chapter title says, I want to talk about the leads being weak.

Many of us can make excuses that "the leads are weak, we don't have customers, the customers we have are tire kickers[8] and lot lizards[9]—they're not looking to buy." But I want you to turn that around and understand something. When I first started out, even when I had a customer who was not a buyer and was just a shopper, I still would try 5, 6, 7, 8, or 9 closing techniques on that person just to gain the experience.

If your customers are waiting in line for you, you're not a closer; you're an order taker. Unless you are knee-deep in sales, make sure you use 100% of that hard, tough close with every person you talk to because you will be surprised. Some of your customers will turn to you and actually buy.

Some customers are just looking or shopping around. Maybe they will shop at several dealerships. But I would still whittle away and bang away at them to try to get the close and improve my closing techniques.

When I say "The Leads Are Weak? You're Weak," I'm referring to Baldwin's funny line in the movie when he says, "I can take the materials that you have and go out and make $15,000—can you?" Here he is alluding to the fact that he could make sales with the bad leads that the sales people were talking about.

Always, always get some form of
   commitment—a deposit, a
   signature on an application,
   something to show their
   commitment.
Ask for it. Ask up front for it and
   don't be afraid.
I don't care how small it is; it's a
   trial close and it gets things
   moving. So many closes go by the
   wayside because you don't get that
   initial opening commitment.

I get that all of the time. Even in my own insurance agency, people will say, "Oh, the leads are weak," or "They're not buyers." Even if that were true, you don't ever want to say that. Even if the leads are awful 100% of the time, work them anyway. Nobody wants to hear the negative, such as, "I just couldn't close them." Work the leads hard again, no matter what, and you will preserve and find some diamonds in the rough. Whenever I went into a client's house, or had someone come to me in the car business, I always did my best to close the customer into something.

For instance, when I was in the car business, I was a top salesman in what we call the Beltway—the area that consists of Maryland, Virginia, and Washington, DC—a really tough car market. Shoppers and buyers are good there. It is a rough location and you really have to be a good closer and good salesman to make a deal.

There are many dealerships there, and you really had to be on your game. Companies used to send what they call shoppers to the dealership to test your sales ability and customer service. Were you good? Did you take care of the customers? Or did you just try to make a sale and blow them out?

I had one customer who I later learned was a shopper. He went through the motions, and I closed him so hard that I made him give me a cash deposit, which I later found out the company gave back to him. That's how hard I want you to close.

When I was in the car business, if a person didn't leave a deposit—$10, $50, or something that I could hold at the desk, with me, or bring to the sales manager's desk—I would not go ahead with the deal. If they didn't come up with something, and I didn't care if it was the keys to their trade-in or a check that was totally refundable if we didn't make a deal, I would not take that deal to the sales manager. Until I got that first signal that he or she would purchase, I did not go any further.

I am the same way today. When I visit someone at home, I look for some kind of commitment, whether it is on paper, an application—something. I will hammer away at a person. Please remember this when you are in a home or if someone comes to you. I am using in-home sales as an example, but certainly you will be out and about if you are in real estate, selling cars, or computer products.

You need to understand that if you're not getting any kind of commitment from that person, you're spinning your wheels— you've got nothing. Always, always get some form of commitment—a deposit, a signature on an application, something to show their commitment. Ask for it. Ask up front for it and don't be afraid. I don't care how small it is; it's a trial close and it gets things moving. So many closes go by the wayside because you don't get that initial opening commitment.

To get that initial commitment, ask these questions:

- Are you ready to own and take delivery of this vehicle?
- Are the figures agreeable?
- Let me ask you a question. Can I go ahead and get an application for you for the life insurance?

Tell your clients how you and the product will work for them.

- If it goes through, you'll have the coverage that you really need to protect your family.
- Give me a deposit on this house, and I'm really going to fight for you.
- I'm really going to work hard for you to go back and make that deal.

As a salesperson, you must relay to that individual that you're going to bat for them. You're going to work for them. You're going to do what you can above and beyond to get them a fair deal.

Isn't that really what everyone wants today? Customers want to feel like they are not being taken—that someone has given them a fair shake. They don't want to feel that someone is taking advantage of them. This is so critical. It is so vital to earn their trust so that you have the right to slam dunk them into the sale. Earn the right to slam dunk them and badger them.

There were times when sitting with someone, I would literally get on top of my desk and scream, "Get out of my dealership or make the sale!" But I earned that right. I didn't do that in the beginning. I went through all of the product knowledge. I gained rapport. I asked clients where they were from, where they went to school, and what kind of work they did. I quickly gathered that information and I battled them on the price.

I would come back to my desk after going back and forth with the sales manager; I would be sweating and they could see the sincerity in my eyes. They could see I was going to battle for them, trying to help them make a deal. And that was the way I thought about it; I wanted to help them. Sure, I wanted to close them hard. I wanted the commission. I needed the money.

But I also made it very clear to everyone that I shook hands with that "I am here to work for you. I'm here to make a deal for you. I'm here to get you the best product—house, car, insurance, computer, timeshare—whatever it is. I'm here for you. I'm here to do the best I can for you."

I know many who are reading this may not be hearing many new ideas. Maybe you're just hearing them in a different way or with a different tone. But so many people fail because they just can't close the deal. They just can't get to a point where they feel comfortable asking for the order. If you're like that, or you're weak in closing, it's not going to work.

In my business, we present seminars, make follow-up appointments, and then go for the close. It's a very effective process. You can be a fantastic public speaker, and be very good on the phone, or maybe great at booking appointments, but once you get face-to-face with your client, if you're not 100% phenomenal at closing, forget it. You're never going to make the big money. I don't care what you're selling.

So, as you read these pages, especially the next several chapters, learn these methods—and learn them well. Some of you may have seen these ideas before; others have not. But the way I present closing is basic and bottom line; you will learn cut-to-the-chase techniques that you must do, and must know how to do in order to close more sales.

I'm very nice and very direct. I don't try to be a *putz*, but I will change the appointment. When I speak to someone, I don't want to belittle him or make him think or say, "What do you mean I can't make a decision without my wife?" I will use other angles, such as telling the customer, "We need to speak to her. I might need her to sign the paperwork."

Chapter 6

*The Only Thing That Counts in This Life Is to Get
Them to Sign on the Line That Is Dotted*

Yes, this title is correct. Let's not mince words. We can tell it any way we want. But until you get them to sign on that bottom line and take delivery of the vehicle, take the product, or initiate some sort of purchase, it's all meaningless.

So, let's begin here. As I said before, I do not spend a lot of time on rapport; I focus on the meat of the close. When you are sitting across the table with someone and you've given this person your information, make sure to do the following:

Number 1: Look directly at them

Look at people directly. Watch them. Watch their eyes. Watch their motions. Notice if they move around in their chair, and so forth. I'm not saying you must become fluent in deciphering body language, but look people in the eye—they appreciate that.

Number 2: Ask for the order

I have often told a salesman that sometimes you will get the sale just by asking. I am going to give you the best example in the world. When I first got involved with insurance, as I mentioned before, I hadn't sold anything for three weeks. I was really ready to give up. I made a follow-up appointment with a gentleman who had heard me at a seminar. He told me that he was not happy with the particular product that he already had.

I said, "Okay. My product can do A, B, C, and D," and I presented it within a very short period of time.

**Make sure you have the ready, able,
    and willing buyer.
Start closing immediately.
"How soon would you like to
    take delivery of the vehicle or
    product?"**

He looked at me and said, "Okay."

I almost froze in my chair. It was a $10,000 commission, and I asked, "What do you mean, 'okay?'" That is when my sales ability took over and I never looked back. He said, "Okay," I froze for a minute, then peeled out that paperwork and got him to sign. I must have gone back to that client's house five or six times because I didn't have the right paperwork and had to get it.

As I've mentioned before, it's fine if you're missing something. It's great for you to go back. It solidifies the sale. I frequently tell agents and salespeople to close the sale and then make up an excuse to go back the next day to do some hand holding to avoid buyer's remorse.

Some of the biggest sales that you will ever make will back-up on you within 48 hours. That's the name of the game. And you'd better be able to stomach it because when you go in, as I will tell you in the various chapters dealing with how to handle buyer's remorse, if you show any sign of weakness, your clients are going to tear you to pieces.

I love going back in on some of the buyer's remorse sales because I solidify the sale and re-close it with confidence. You must be ready for buyer's remorse, going back in, and re-closing the sale. Oftentimes these buyers will turn out, in the long run, to be the best clients you've ever had.

It's a numbers game. If you're going to three or four appointments each day, you're going to sell one just by asking for the order. There's an old saying, "A broken clock still works twice a day." In your initiation, always ask for the sale. You'll be surprised how many times you'll get a "Yes!"

If only life would be so easy and everyone would say "Yes!" I certainly wouldn't be writing this book, and salesmen would basically just be order takers. But those situations are few and far between. Just always have the mindset that they are going to say "Yes!" because this does happen from time to time and you want to be prepared for it.

Number 3: Beware of lies and embellishments

The bottom line is buyers sometimes lie. I'm not saying this to insult buyers. I'm not saying they are looking to take advantage of someone. On the contrary, as I've said before, people just don't want to feel like they are being taken.

Buyers are going to put on what some old closers used to call a brick overcoat.[10] They are going to embellish or misrepresent the truth a little, or out-and-out lie. They are going to tell you, "I can get a better deal at So-and-So. The price was better over there. Their service was better or they offered me more." They are going to do that. I don't pay any attention to these comments. I actually don't even hear them. When they tell you things like this, just let these remarks go through.

Let me be clear here because I am a good listener. I do make people feel comfortable and make them feel that I am sincere. But with regards to closing, when they tell me they can get A, B, C, or D, many times it is a smoke screen,[11] and I will continue to close, and close hard, just to go through the smoke. If it is a real objection, it will stop a sale at the end.

If it's a real objection where they say, "Look, I have, in writing, a better price from So-and-So down the street; here it is. I'm just not going to buy from you. I think you're the nicest guy in the world, but I'm not going to buy from you unless you match or beat that rate," that is something different. But lot of times they're just embellishing.

I once had a situation in my car sales career where somebody came to me and said, "Someone bought from this dealership at this price." It was absolutely impossible that they could get a car at that price.

I said, "Look, Mrs. Jones, most people, when you talk to them, will embellish a little bit. How many times do you say to your neighbor, 'Oh, you bought that nice Honda. How much did you pay for it?'"

"'Oh, around $28,000 they'll tell you. They'll usually drop the figure several thousand dollars. He really paid $33,000, but everyone embellishes."

So I obtained the name of the buyer the customer was referring to, went into company records, and returned with the buyer's order. I showed the customer what the other buyer really paid for the car and said, "Look, I'm giving you the same deal," and I made the deal.

Number 4: Engage the Silent Client

Let's assume I've given a presentation and the buyer doesn't just say "Yes!" This time, the buyer says nothing. Have you ever been in a situation where a client says nothing the whole time? Sometimes these are actually the worst buyers because at the end of the presentation they are just going to tell you, "I just want to think about it."

You want to engage buyers. You want to bring them into the conversation. You want to get the objections out of the buyers. If they say, "I'm not interested. I don't want to do business today," at least you have something. When people just sit there and shake their heads, they are usually the tougher buyers to close.

By the way, I speak Yiddish. I speak *tachliss* and *emet*—frankly and truthfully. I'm not going to sit here and tell you every one of my closing techniques will nail a deal every time. It's far from that.

You're going to be in situations where people are just not going to buy. There are three things to keep in mind to make a close. You must have a ready, willing, and able buyer. You must have someone who has an interest in the product. You must have someone who is willing, and he must have the capacity to buy.

Besides having the capacity to buy, is *he* the actual buyer? Smoke out that situation early on in your presentation. "Is there anyone else who is going to help you make this decision?" Don't go through a 30-minute presentation and find out, "Oh, I have to ask my husband," or whatever.

The one thing that I learned very early on is to not do a presentation if someone tells me, "I make all of the decisions; my wife is not around." I will simply change the appointment and in a very nice way say, "I have to go over the information with her and may have to have her on the application as a beneficiary." Whatever you want to say, change the appointment.

I got burned on that one and I'll never forget it. I walked into a house and the husband said, "Sit down. You don't need my wife. I make every f—king decision. You sell me on the product." I sat in that home for 45 minutes and gave him the best presentation of my life, and at the end he said, "Okay, now I have to talk to my wife."

I won't do it anymore. If I anger the customer and he doesn't reschedule the appointment, that's okay. I was basically going to have nothing anyway.

I'm very nice and very direct. I don't try to be a *putz* (Yiddish for idiot or fool), but I will change the appointment. When I speak to someone, I don't want to belittle him or make him think or say, "What do you mean I can't make a decision without my wife?" I will use other angles, such as telling the customer, "We need to speak to her. I might need her to sign the paperwork."

Make sure you have the ready, able, and willing buyer. Start closing immediately. "How soon would you like to take delivery of the vehicle or product?"

Once you have this commitment, you must close, and I mean hard. In today's times, salespeople are a dime a dozen and you have to whittle away at your clients. You have to remove that brick overcoat in a nice way until they go along with what you're talking about. If you have a good product and good presentation, you will start getting them to sign the paperwork.

If you've read other sales books and you're reading mine, you know that small, trial closes work. "May I have your social security number? May I see your driver's license?" You can try these little trial closes, and close, close, close.

So always, always be closing, from beginning to end. We will get into objections and more closing techniques. Just keep focusing on closing. You want to become a mega-closer.

Chapter 7

ABC—Always Be Closing

Always, always be closing. When you are in the process of closing a sale, or you're meeting and greeting a client and providing product descriptions, as you are talking you want to be closing the people on that sale.

You've met them. You've greeted them. You've already discussed the different products with them. And now you are sitting at the table with them. Again, we are most concerned with the closing, the objections you are going to get, and how to handle them.

You've shown the product and you've asked for the order— "Would you like to move forward? Would you like to take delivery today?" It's critical that you ask for the order. As I mentioned before, so many deals are lost for simply not asking for the sale.

You've asked. They've said "No."

Let's run down the objections again:

- I want to think about it.
- I've got to talk to a friend of mine.
- I've got to talk to my aunt or uncle.
- I need some time.
- I want to go around to a different dealership.
- I'd like to get a second opinion.

Let's run down the objections again:
- **I want to think about it.**
- **I've got to talk to a friend of mine.**
- **I've got to talk to my aunt or uncle.**
- **I need some time.**
- **I want to go to a different dealership.**
- **I'd like to get a second opinion.**

Most of these objections are smoke screens. They are situations where someone is saying to you, "I don't trust you and I'm not ready to do business with you."

Most of these objections are smoke screens. They are situations where someone is saying to you, "I don't trust you and I'm not ready to do business with you."

I've already given you some lines to smoke out these objections in the beginning, such as, "Is there anyone else who will be helping you make this decision?" So, let's assume you have gone through the presentation and you didn't get any adverse reactions from the buyers. They didn't give you anything else that would say to you that they wouldn't want to buy.

Now that you have hit them directly with "Are you ready to own and take delivery of this product today?" you get "I want to think about it." That answer isn't good enough. I'll come back with my normal line, "Oh, I appreciate that. That's great that you want to think about it, but before we finish up today, just to satisfy my curiosity, what is it that you would like to think about?"

"What is it that you want to think about?" always works. Sometimes I get my briefcase as if I am going away, which really catches them off guard. I'll say, "Okay—no problem. I'm going to see another client today, but before I leave, I'm just curious; what is it that you want to think about?" Normally, they will produce whatever the objection is, and I will produce an answer to that objection.

In addition, when I've gone over the product and I'm ready to close, if the buyers are husband and wife, I'll excuse myself for a minute. I'll go out and let them actually discuss the situation. I've had people in sales tell me going out to give them time is the biggest mistake in the world; if the buyers want to get out of the sale or are just not interested, this gives them the opportunity to do that.

Here's what I do. I go over some of the details. I don't hammer them hard. We've sat down, and now I'm saying, "I'd like to work for you. I'd like to deliver this product to you. Give me a second." And I'll go away.

To excuse myself if I am in their home, I will tell them I need to get some papers from my car. If you're in a situation where you are on a sales floor, you can easily get up and say, "I want to check on something for you." Let me tell you what giving them time to talk alone has done for me—it has worked magic.

"What is it that you want to think about?"
  always works.

Sometimes I get my briefcase as if I am
  going away, which really catches them
  off guard. I'll say, "Okay—no problem.
  I'm going to see another client today,
  but before I leave, I'm just curious;
  what is it that you want to think about?"
  Normally, they will produce whatever
  the objection is, and I will produce an
  answer to that objection.

When you leave, they are going to say one of two things to each other. They may say, "I like this, honey, let's go ahead and go with it when he comes back," or "Oh, good—now that we've seen him, I don't like this guy; no matter what he says, we're not buying."

Their private discussion really sets the tone for what you have. If you had tried to stand on them to close and they really didn't want your product, you'll just get a refund request, complaint, a comeback, or a cancellation—however you have it spelled out in your sales.

When I return to the table with my paperwork, I'll say, "So, let's take a look at this." Normally, they will tell me what they discussed. I may hear, "Oh, Larry, we really like the product. If you can get it for us like this, we'll take it." Or they may say, "Oh, Larry, while you were away, we decided that we really want to think about this."

With the second answer, "We really want to think about this," I know they are really not ready to buy, and I will hammer them with the "think about it" close. But I may also have the situation where no matter what I do, I will not be able to close them.

I have found that this technique really cuts through the process. As I've said all along, when I'm in a home, I'm there to do business. I'm not there to *schmooze* for 30-45 minutes. I'm there to cut to the chase, to be nice, to be informative, to see where I'm at, and get a commitment. Sometimes I'll be in a home and use this technique after only 10 minutes because I quickly see there are issues going on between the husband and wife during the presentation.

Again, always leave the customers alone for a minute or two because it will reap you benefits. The bad news is that this technique can only show you when you come back that you don't have buyers; they will do everything they can to weasel out of the sale. Or, the good news—when you come back, they will be in unison, and you can make adjustments and move forward to close the deal.

Let's use a $500,000 policy as an example of this. I've returned to the buyers and they've said, "I think we are more interested in getting a $125,000 policy." If I never gave them time to speak to each other alone, this information—what they could afford—may never have been revealed and the deal could have been lost.

The same thing applies to the car business. If I go away and they've said to themselves, "I want to go with him, but I don't want to go more than $350 on the car payment," they are both on the same page. When I return and they've told me this, I can then adjust the terms and close the deal. Again, this method either gets them on the same page for you having a deal, or it leaves you having nothing.

Use this technique; it is very critical. When you come back to the buyers to hammer away with "Are you ready to buy?" or "Are you ready to do business today?" you will get your answers. Your buyers will come back with an objection and you will handle it, or you will move forward with a sale.

Chapter 8

You Close or You Hit the Bricks

In the previous chapter I gave you some tips on closing and what to do. Now, let's talk about closing hard and getting through objections.

I've already given you some responses to objections such as, "I'd like to think about it." My comeback, word for word is, "Mr. So-and-So, what is it that you really need to think about, just to satisfy my own curiosity?"

Let's go further. Many times a buyer will answer, "I want to talk to someone about it." How do you close when you get this objection? At this point I will ask, "Are you satisfied with the product and the presentation?"

If they tell me they want to discuss it with certain people, they are blowing smoke. When this happens, I will to say to them, "Are you ready to own and take delivery? Are you ready to sign today if the figures and numbers are agreeable? Are you ready to move forward with this contract if all of the numbers and everything work out okay?"

Remember, I have already asked them these questions when I sat with them during my presentation. Normally, I've set all of that up front. It's a lot of BS if they tell me, "I want to think about it. I want to talk to someone. The price is too high. I want to speak to my neighbor. I want to speak to my attorney. I want to shop."

With all of these objections, I basically come back with the same answers every time. "Oh, just to satisfy my curiosity, why is

With all of these objections, I basically
   come back with the same answers
   every time.
"Oh, just to satisfy my curiosity, why
   is it that you want to speak to this
   person?"
"By the way, that is interesting. Why
   do you want to go and do that?"

it that you want to speak to this person? By the way, that is interesting. Why do you want to go and do that?"

I just ask them directly—looking right into their eyes—and then I'll continue my closing, "Based on that, if they say it's a go, why don't we go ahead and put the figures together now, and let's write this up."

I will just continue, continue to move forward. I will look at that person again, and I don't mean in a mean way or a way that they will say, "Oh my God, this guy won't leave us alone." I call it "back door closing"—subtly saying over and over again, "Oh, I like what you're saying. Sure, go ahead and think about it. In the meantime, let's get you on paper and let's start to get this written up. We can always talk to So-and-So on the phone. We can make a phone call."

People who I am talking to now and who are reading my book may have already bought books about closing techniques. Zig Ziglar and Tom Hopkins have very good information; they will give you lists upon lists of typical types of closures to use with your customers. I'm trying to give you closing the hardball way. Have three, four, or five different closes under your belt.

More importantly, what I want to get across in this book is that you must be able to close hard. If you don't close—if you don't keep going and going and going, like the Energizer battery—you're not going to get them.

Sometimes people need closings to be repeated 10 or 15 times. They don't need 10 or 15 types of closes. They just need you to go back again and again and again. Try to look at it as though you are sitting across from them playing a video game like "Space Invaders"[12] or something stronger. You're firing away, firing to knock down their shield. You are whaling away at their brick overcoat, to knock that down and expose them in a nice way and in a good way. Once they're exposed, they can be closed.

I want you to always remember that line. Once they're exposed, they can be closed. That's what you have to constantly do, over and over and over again, to close the deal.

You're going to find many times in your sales career that you make a great sale only to find the client wants to cancel the next

Sometimes people need closings to be repeated 10 or 15 times. They don't need 10 or 15 types of closes. They just need you to go back again and again and again. Try to look at it as though you are sitting across from them playing a video game like "Space Invaders" or something stronger. You're firing away, firing to knock down their shield. You are whaling away at their brick overcoat, to knock that down and expose them in a nice way and in a good way. Once they're exposed, they can be closed.

day. Actually, this is a good thing if they call you to cancel. If they go over your head or go directly, let's say, to the insurance company or manufacturer, you don't get the chance to re-close. So what do you do if the buyer calls the next day to cancel? I am going to give you my secret which, when used properly, will often save the sale and reduce your buyer's remorse cancellations, resulting in a large increase in your income.

The first thing you do is tell them that there is no problem with this and you're sorry to hear that they want to cancel. Then make an appointment to see them. Sometimes they will try to get out of this, but say you are bringing them a form to sign off on the cancellation. Tell them you want them to sign off on a form canceling the policy so there are no issues down the road. I don't want someone saying they never canceled a policy. I want it in writing.

Now, here's the key. When you meet them, have the cancellation letter on your desk or bring it out immediately if you're at their home or place of business. This will diffuse any thoughts they may have that you are not sincere or are really there to re-close. Ask them to sign the form and say exactly this: "Gee, just out of curiosity, because this happens so infrequently with me, why are you canceling?"

Now watch and listen, because nine times of ten they will tell you the real reason and you can re-close the sale. Having them sign the letter is gutsy but it will get to the real objection. I have torn up many letters like that after I got the real objection and re-closed. Even when I re-close them, I say that I will still hold onto the letter if they get cold feet again, and, of course, this rarely happens.

This works because it's non-threatening. If you try and just re-close without knowing what's really going on, you will lose the sale. Remember, you work for them, so show you're sincere and show them that you mean business and if they want to cancel, that's fine. I once had a million dollar sale cancel on me and I used this method. Once they signed the cancellation letter that day, I didn't even try to re-close. Two days later they called me to say they never had anyone be so nice during a cancellation and not try and pressure them back into the sale. They figured my product must be good, and I made the sale after all.

Again, when clients or customers try to cancel, it can be a blessing. It's a way to get to the real issues, giving you the opportunity to overcome their objections and re-close the sale. Use this tactic exactly as given and it will work wonders for you.

Chapter 9

A Guy Don't Walk on the Lot, 'Less He Wants to Buy!

There is a fantastic book that you should read—*100 Ways to Create Wealth* by Steve Chandler and Sam Beckford. It's about motivation, creating wealth, and sales.

This book has a line that is so true. In fact, I really thought these words were mine until I read them in this book. They talk about products with commissions from $3,000–$300,000 and the fear you may have selling the higher ticket items.

To get over the fear, they tell you to just move the decimal point over. I've talked about this many times in sales seminars and in all of my sales training. One of the keys to my success was my being able to go to a client, whether for an estate planning deal for a million dollars or only several thousand dollars, and have the same peaceful feeling, as the book says, asking for the higher amounts.

So many people have that fear and say, "I'd like to be able to sell the larger home, the larger product, or do a bigger job, but I get nervous about it."

This fear will crush you every time. When you walk into someone's home or they come to you, no matter how much they're worth, you must have the attitude that people are people. If you're giving your clients the highest possible quality of service, and in your heart you know you are really doing a good job for them, it doesn't matter.

We've talked a little about the old sayings, "Oh, he just wanted to think about it. He's a tire kicker. He's a lot lizard. He's just

This fear will crush you every time. When you walk into someone's home or they come to you, no matter how much they're worth, you must have the attitude that people are people. If you're giving your clients the highest possible quality of service, and in your heart you know you are really doing a good job for them, it doesn't matter.

shopping." Again, it doesn't matter. People come into businesses and may say, "I'm just looking. I don't want to buy until next year. I just want to pick up a brochure."

That person, that lot lizard, has an interest in the product, and it is up to you to create what I call sales urgency. "Oh, you aren't interested in a car? You just want to pick up a brochure for six months from now? What, are you kidding me with the way car and gas prices are going? They are going to be way up. Right now, we have some phenomenal deals." Or, "Oh, the real estate market is down? Are you kidding me? Come on, you are going to get the best possible price imaginable right now."

I am very good at this—turning a real sales negative into a positive, and you really have to get good at this, too. Here's an example. When you are working with a customer and you have his interest and are ready to close, what happens when he starts coming back with comments such as, "I did do business with you a number of years ago and the service stunk. The salesman stunk, or this or that was bad"? You must turn it around.

There is a famous book called *The Closers* by Ben Gay III. It gives lots of different closes and objection responses. I've used one of their methods for many years to counter objections and turn the situation around.

I look the client in the eye and say, "You know, we had that situation, and what do you think we did about it?" Or you can put a spin on it, as some books suggest, and say, "You know, Mr. Jones, what would you do if you owned this dealership, and they were giving you poor service and you had the opportunity to do something about it?"

Normally, Mr. Jones is going to say, "I'd change it. I'd fire the guy. I'd get some new help." And I respond, "Well, that's exactly what we did. And now our service is better."

I'm always able to take a negative, turn it around, and close. You will see a lot of sales books talking about handling these objections. When you spin that objection into a positive, it is critical to make sure you turn around and ask for the sale and stay on him.

I've always found that when I get an objection while closing, I need to come back twice as hard. For example, your client says, "Well, I've got to think about it."

When someone asks, "Can I get that in black?" you should respond, "Will you take that in black?" These are all good tag lines. Keep in mind one thing—you're coming back hard against any type of buying signal. When you hear, "Oh, gee, can I get this in black," don't just say, "Oh, would you like that in black?" Tell them, "Yes, we can get it in black. Let's go ahead and get the paperwork going."

I respond, "What is it that you want to think about?"

He tells me what he wants to think about and boom—I close hard and ask him for the sale. I cannot stress this enough.

I've said this throughout this book and it is critical. Any time you come back to the client with something, such as a talk with your sales manager if you're in the car industry or another business, you need to say, "I'll see if I can get you that, and once we get you that, of course we have a deal, is that correct?"

This applies even if you're the owner of the business and the buck stops there. If you own a business or you're in sales or you're a manager, always use the excuse that you have to talk to someone else. It has always helped me out if someone said to me, "Look, I'm willing to go with you, but can you just do this little bit more?"

Instead of just sitting there and saying, "Yeah, I can do that," and let them think I have money on the table, I will always tell the client, "Let me make a phone call. Let me call home office. Let me do this or that, and I'll see if I can get you that, and once we get you that, of course we have a deal, is that correct?" The answer will most often be "Yes."

You'll see this in a lot of sales literature—question for question. When someone asks, "Can I get that in black?" you should respond, "Will you take that in black?" These are all good tag lines. Keep in mind one thing—you're coming back hard against any type of buying signal. When you hear, "Oh, gee, can I get this in black," don't just say, "Oh, would you like that in black?" Tell them, "Yes we can get it in black. Let's go ahead and get the paperwork going."

Follow my lead as you read this entire book about closing. It's talking about getting into a client's head and just continually, be it soft or be it sometimes hard, closing. Take every person who comes in, look at them, work them, and work them hard—even if they're tire tickers, even if you really, really believe you've seen them around before and they're BSers. You'll be surprised. Once in awhile, one of them comes around.

The salesman who thinks, "Oh, he's just a tire kicker," says, "How are you doing? Here's our brochure," and then lets a customer go, isn't doing the job. A customer may come around at a later date, so treat everyone right.

If one of them comes around once a month, whether your average commission ticket is $500 or $10,000, that could be an extra $6,000-$120,000 per year. Work them over. Close them hard enough so that if they are just tire kickers, they'll think twice about coming back.

Chapter 10

I Used to Be a Salesman—It's a Tough Racket

A lot of people are no longer in this business, and they were at one time. Being in sales can really have its ups and downs. When you meet people in sales, of course you have to be positive. But salesmen are moody.

Let's face it. Salesmen come home at night. They didn't make a sale that day. They're crabby. Sometimes they just want to go into their room. Sometimes they just don't want to talk. Sometimes it's the opposite; they want to go out, tie one on for the evening, and forget about it.

But salesmen are a very unique breed. As a matter of fact, when you're selling someone, it's very, very intimate. You really get to know that person. Many times you find salespeople will create a relationship with someone they have sold and then actually turn it into a friendship because for that short period of time, no matter how long that sale lasts, you develop a close, friendly relationship.

My father was a very successful real estate attorney who worked his way up, paid his way through college and law school— a real success story. He came out of the depression. I remember when he passed away very young—at 62. I was only 16 at the time and I really struggled with that—losing him so young.

I remember hearing stories from my father. He talked about the job he had as a credit manager for a department store. This would have been around the 1930s, and he always spoke about how he really got to know people based on their credit and by talking to

Let the client win some victories.
Show respect. "Oh, you did this? You
did that business? Wow—that must
have been exciting." A guy could tell
me anything. He could say "I sell
caskets" and I could put a spin on it
and answer, "Gee, I never knew
anyone who did that. How does that
work when somebody comes in to buy
a casket? What do you offer them
first? What do most people buy?"

them and doing a little bit of selling. It's so true. When you're selling someone something, you really get to know what type of person he is.

When I was about 17 or 18, maybe a year after I lost my father, I was going through his library; a lot of his books from the law firm were brought to our house and just put in the basement. One of the books that stuck out was *How to Win Friends and Influence People* by Dale Carnegie. *How to Stop Worrying and Start Living*, also by Carnegie, was another.

I've read those books over and over again, probably for the last 30 years, and they work. *How to Win Friends and Influence* People really delves into how to win over people, and that has always been successful for me.

When I go into a home, I don't care what type the people are. Just being a kind person, walking in, and saying, "How are you doing? Where are you from? How did you grow up? How did you become successful?" is important. I do this especially if I want to get into them and to get some more information from them.

There's an old saying, "Talk to a person about himself and he will listen for hours." If you hit the right button, most people will be willing to talk about themselves for a long period of time.

Again, you know that I don't go in and *schmooze* for hours and hours. But I do know how to go in and, in a very short time, get to know that person and try to understand him. You want to understand him. You want to think like him. You want to get into his mind and know exactly what he's thinking.

And, as you do this, be sincere. Ask questions. Qualify him. Let him tell the stories and anecdotes about how he built his business and what line of work he's in. That always works. Let him talk.

What is he thinking about? Why would he want to buy this life insurance? What's really in it for him? Is it just that if something happens to him, he wants to make sure he provides for his wife? Maybe that's not entirely it. Maybe he wants enough for his kids. Maybe, in his heart, he's got a partner in business, and he doesn't want that partner to be troubled financially by his death.

As funny as it may sound, people sometimes want insurance for reasons you don't realize—for protection, out of fear, because of their money concepts. What is their fear? Why would they want to

Review my chapter about walking outside, taking some pressure off, and then walking back in and closing hard again. You have to be the judge when you're with that person. You have to take his temperature as to how far you can, in a nice way, push.

buy these investments from you? What I'm saying to you is, get into their head.

Let me give you another example—how I've acquired single family homes over the years. Normally, I do business with someone selling their own home. I walk through the house and in the 10 – 15 minutes that I walk through that house, I'm able to ask the owner questions. I'm able to ask him things about his life—where he grew up, what he did—to where I've bonded with him.

You'd be very surprised what that bonding does. At the end of that 15 minute conversation, I'm able to look at him and ask, "Are you able to take on some owner financing? Would you reduce the price more? " I'm able to look in his eye. Many times, not all the time, but the times when the person has turned around and said, "Yeah, I'll make a deal with you," were based on them liking me.

I'll tell you about another experience I had. I've leased cars over the years; I can't stand paying for them and paying all those fees. People can have their leases taken over now. For example, if someone has leased a car with Mercedes, you can actually apply for the car and transfer that lease for a few hundred dollars.

I happened to find a beautiful, white BMW 7 Series located in my area. I saw it advertised on the Internet and called the person. I said, "I'm local. I'm in Boca Raton, and you're in Boca. Can I look at the car?"

I went to the look at the vehicle. He had other lookers and tire kickers and I could see that he was a little negative. I loved the car and there were only ten months left on the lease. It was perfect for me because I go through cars very quickly. I put a lot of mileage on them and, the truth is, I'm sick of them after ten months. We established rapport and I had asked him, "What do you do?"

He had a business overseas and some local real estate that we talked about, and we actually became a little friendly afterwards. I came back to him with an offer—I would pay up the lease for the ten months and would give the payment to him over a 90-120 day period.

We went back and forth; he wasn't sure about this and that. I talked to him and we sent emails back and forth. I had my attorney draw up a small contract and fax it over to him, and he finally said, "Okay, I think I might go for that." I met him, signed the paperwork, and drove off—zero money down as far as I'm concerned.

Here's the point. After we made the deal, we got a little friendly. One day I called him up; he had a property I wanted to look at. When I picked him up and he got in the car, he said, "You know, I like you—and that's the reason I made this deal. I would not have made it for anybody else. A lot of people came here, and I really didn't care; I wasn't interested. But you took an interest in me, and I appreciated that. Actually, I liked you, and that's why I made the deal."

All through this book, you hear me talking about two things—establishing rapport quickly, and closing hard. I have a few more comments on establishing rapport. It doesn't have to take a long time, but you want to get into his head where he really, truly believes that you are sincere.

The second, the nanosecond, that a customer decides that you're not trustworthy, or you don't have his best interests at heart, I don't' care how many times you try to close him, you're going to fail. And that's okay. It's okay if you fail, because not everyone is going to like you. But I don't want you to fail because you didn't know how to close. If, however, you are losing a lot of sales because the customer just didn't like you, it means you are not establishing a nice rapport or doing it very well.

I'm talking about closing hard in this book. And yes, I'm talking about slam dunking these people. But what I'm also telling you is—earn that right. Be kind to them in the beginning. Establish rapport and be sincere. "Wow, you did that?"

Joe Girard always talks about establishing common ground in his books. Let the client win some victories. Show respect. "Oh, you did this? You did that business? Wow—that must have been exciting." A guy could tell me anything. He could say "I sell caskets" and I could put a spin on it and answer, "Gee, I never knew anyone who did that. How does that work when somebody comes in to buy a casket? What do you offer them first? What do most people buy?"

The guy will talk for hours about his business. I don't care what it is. Again, turn around and slam dunk him. That's how you do it.

And that's how you've got to keep doing it to succeed in the sales game. And it's hard—it's very, very hard.

Many times you'll run into people who will give you that old *Glengarry Glen Ross* line, "Yeah, I used to be a salesman—it's a tough racket." You know what? That's why the rewards are so big. Why do you think people are so jealous of salesmen? There are certain products in the insurance business that many people try to denigrate. One of the reasons for this is the lucrative commissions.

The truth is, in sales you can starve. You might have something with a big commission, and you may only sell it once a year. For someone who sells commercial real estate, it can take two years to make a deal, but they make themselves $125,000.

If you are struggling, read my book word for word, and close hard. I don't care if you anger someone once in awhile. Maybe they'll get upset and they'll look at you and say, "You know, you're pressuring me a little too much." But, if you follow my lines, if you follow my closing techniques, you can earn that right to close him hard, and close him without him thinking that you're a pushy, pushy person.

Review my chapter about walking outside, taking some pressure off, and then walking back in and closing hard again. You have to be the judge when you're with that person. You have to take his temperature as to how far you can, in a nice way, push.

But I'd rather push hard and have someone feel I'm pushing him too much and walk out the door than be thinking, "Maybe, if I'd have tried one or two more closes, I'd have gotten him." Don't ever feel that way. Don't ever let a guy walk out and then think, "You know, I could have had him."

When I first started in sales, whatever type of product I sold, that always happened. After I became successful with a particular product, I always looked back and said, "You know, I remember that guy; I remember that couple. Had I used what I know now, I would have gotten them."

There's no sense in regretting what you didn't know before. If you are experienced right now, pick up the closing techniques, and close hard. If you're reading my book and you're new to sales, you will miss some in the beginning. All I am saying, especially if you are new at this game, is learn closing, and you can end up being a more successful salesperson in 90 days than someone who has a lot more experience.

I proved that. When I first got into the car business, I had never sold cars in my life, but within 90 days I was the number one salesman at that dealership. I was probably number one in the Mid-Atlantic region. They never really calculated, but I had gone to different dealerships and saw the numbers. I was selling between 20–30 cars per month, which, belly-to-belly, was big in itself.

When I was in insurance sales, I used to be in the top ten in the country each year—those were belly-to-belly sales. Many times in the insurance business, a guy could sell and also have agents under him for which he could sign off and get the credit.

We had agents under us, but my personal, individual sales were one-on-one. And I was victorious, year after year, being in the top ten in the country. I'm not talking about 5,000, 10,000, or 20,000 agents. One year, I was number seven in a company of 140,000 agents alone, not even counting the other insurance companies in the country.

Chapter 11

You Think This Is Abuse?

There's a very famous line in *Glengarry Glen Ross* where the sales manager, Alec Baldwin, says to Alan Arkin, "You think this is abuse? If you think this is abuse, how can you take the abuse on an appointment?"

This is absolutely fantastic because it is saying you'd better learn *before* you hit the streets, *before* you go on the appointment. Learn everything you can about that product and how to sell it.

When I was in sales, I role played for years. I asked family and friends to be the worst possible client or customer that they could be so that I could learn from that situation and learn to take the abuse. Then when I was with a client, it was easy.

Practice role playing with your wife, a friend, a girlfriend, or a boyfriend, and run through those hard, heavy duty objections. Then it's easy when you're out on an appointment or you're with someone you're trying to close.

When I was in the car business, I was more afraid of the sales managers than the customers. I went into meetings with them and came out chewed up. They told me, "You'd better go out and hammer that client. You'd better make that sale, or you're out of here."

That lit a fire under my rear, and I'll tell you something: if you're in a business where you don't have a sales manager like that, or you don't have someone over you pushing you, then you'd better push yourself. You'd better get motivated to get out there and close, and close hard.

When I was in sales, I role played for
years; I asked family and friends to be
the worst possible client or customer
that they could be so that I could
learn from that situation and learn to
take the abuse. Then when I was with
a client, it was easy.

The abuse I used to get in the sales meetings, or sometimes from the one-on-one with the sales manager or general manager, was oftentimes a lot worse than what I got from the client.

There is another great motivational book by Steve Chandler that I suggest you read—*100 Ways to Motivate Yourself.* Chandler made a very good point about an experience he had with a Little League game. The team they were up against pitched very, very hard and his team members were very nervous. So, instead of using the regular ball during their practice sessions, he used small golf balls, or something similar, that he was able to throw much harder. The team trained with the golf balls and when it came time for the game, the other team's pitching actually seemed a little slower.

It is a brilliant concept, and it goes along with sales. If you have people who will help you practice getting pummeled by a customer or client in a re-enactment, acting, or a practice session, it's much easier than when you are in those closes. When I did seminars for my insurance business, I got up in front of a mirror and literally practiced for a solid hour until I got it perfect, even if my speech was only 20 minutes long.

When you know your business and you know your closes, it's a powerful thing. When you get a person who says, "I'll take it. Sign me up. Write me up," what a feeling of energy!

There's a great group interview scene in the 2000 movie *Boiler Room*, written and directed by Ben Younger. I love the line when Ben Affleck says, "You think money can't buy happiness? Well, look at the f—in' smile on my face!" A lot of these different sales movies talk about this. You don't have to go out and watch all these movies. As I've said before, you can Google *Glengarry Glen Ross*, Alec Baldwin, and Ben Affleck (as Jim Young) in *Boiler Room*, and these scenes will come up. Another film I liked a lot was Oliver Stone's and Stanley Weiser's 1987 film *Wall Street* with Michael Douglas.

These guys are cocky. They're in movies and they're good motivators. I recently read where Phil Jackson of the Los Angeles Lakers played the Alec Baldwin scene from *Glengarry Glen Ross* before one of their big playoff games—and they won! Watching great actors in these inspiring films will help you get pumped up.

When I did seminars for my insurance business, I got up in front of a mirror and literally practiced for a solid hour until I got it perfect, even if my speech was only 20 minutes long.

I want you to understand there's nothing wrong with wanting to make money—with wanting to make lots of money. There's nothing wrong with being in sales if you're doing the right thing. It's strong. It's okay to make that money on sales. We work hard and are commission-based only. That's why we're paid for the big numbers.

Show me someone who is in a sales business such as retail, where they pay you a weekly salary plus a bonus, and I'll show you someone who will never make the six figures. They can't do it. They can't guarantee high salaries plus big commissions. The way to do that is, of course, by us salespeople taking that risk. Commend yourself. Pat yourself on the back if you're a salesman out there.

I know a lot of you picking up this book are probably good closers. Maybe you own a home. Maybe you're closing 20%, 30%, or 40%, but I will guarantee you that with my book, you will close an additional 20%—and that's very conservative. Depending upon what you're selling, if you are earning a commission of $10,000 each month, and you're getting 20% more, that's an extra $2,000 per month, or $24,000 each year. Even if it's only an extra $500, and that's monthly, that's an extra $6,000 per year.

In the end, be willing to take abuse—on the sit or in practice. If I'm in a sit, I'll take as much abuse as possible if I come out with a check, a sale, or a commitment. You'd better do the same thing. And if you're reading my book, you'd better start closing hard—now! No one is going to give you anything in this world. I'm not trying to get on a high horse and try to be "Mr. Motivator," but if you don't close it, nobody is going to do it for you. That's the real meaning here.

When you learn some of these closing techniques and actually go out and do it, take the credit. Nobody helped you. You took these ideas and you closed and you closed hard. You're making a nice living. You're earning an income. That's all on you. Be very proud of yourself.

What I've found over the years is the most successful people aren't necessarily the most talented. They are the ones who keep plugging away. They are the ones who fall down and get up, and continue—continue to press for that sale, to meet and greet people.

Chapter 12

The Final Close

We've talked a lot about closing in these chapters, and I know it isn't as easy as it says or reads. I've been down before. I've been up, and I've been down, and I know what it's like in the trenches.

I know what it's like when you just can't seem to get that sale or you're discouraged. What I've found over the years is the most successful people aren't necessarily the most talented. They are the ones who keep plugging away. They are the ones who fall down and get up, and continue—continue to press for that sale, to meet and greet people.

If you're in a situation where you're just not closing on one or two appointments a day, get a third appointment. That extra daily appointment amounts to an extra five each week—20 per month. And if you close 10% or 20%, that is an extra two to four sales that could make a difference.

You must learn to focus. Claude M. Bristol, in his ground-breaking book *The Magic of Believing*, talks about getting in front of a mirror to practice and focus. I mentioned this in a previous chapter. Do this not only for your seminars and sales techniques. Get up in the morning, stand in front of a mirror, and talk about your dreams and goals.

There's a famous rabbi, Rabbi Nachman of Breslov, who talked about praying and asking for help in your own words. *The Gentle Weapon: Prayers for Everyday and Not-so-Everyday Moments: Timeless Wisdom* from Rebbe Nachman of Breslov discusses this.

**If you believe in a Higher Power, talk
to Him. Talk in normal terms and
from your heart—not worrying about
prayer books, certain forms of
religion, or how to do it specifically.
Just say how you feel. If you're down
and having a rough time, talk about it
with your Higher Power. Pray about
it. Ask for help and you will find a
Spiritual Source. We all go through
this. We all have our tough times.**

If you believe in a Higher Power, talk to Him. Talk in normal terms and from your heart—not worrying about prayer books, certain forms of religion, or how to do it specifically. Just say how you feel. If you're down and having a rough time, talk about it with your Higher Power. Pray about it. Ask for help and you will find a Spiritual Source. We all go through this. We all have our tough times.

Commend yourself if you're a salesperson. Pat yourself on the back. Do you know why? It is a tough racket. A lot of guys don't make it. But how rewarding is it when you make that sale, when you shake their hand and close them? It's a victory. You're triumphant on the battle field. You've made the sale. You've done the right thing for the client. You're going to make a nice commission.

I am emphatic in this book, and I use a lot of different techniques from *Glengarry Glen Ross*. It was a very tough situation in that meeting where Alec Baldwin cussed people out and told them they were no good. I don't mean to come off in a harsh way. I've been a very successful salesman by doing the right thing, treating people right, and treating people well. But I've used what I call the *Glengarry* tactics because sometimes you need, as I've said previously, to light a fire under your own rear end. And *Glengarry Glen Ross* does that.

ABC—remember that. Always be closing. Think about that all day as you're talking to people. When we come in contact with people during the day, aren't we all closing them for something?

Unfortunately, that's the way life is. In life, a lot of us have to sell or be sold. But you know what? It can be fun. It can be exciting. It can be exhilarating. I love to get something in the mail—a bill or something that needs adjustment—just so that I can call that person and close about getting a reduction or making it better for me.

I'm able to get that adjustment or sale because I make the other guy feel good. I'm going to close hard on this case and really stay on him until I get him. But I'm going to do it the right way—the honest way. I'm going to get into his head. I'm going to do a good job for him. You do the same thing.

Remember to follow my words "to a T." By the time you finish this book, you will be prepared to close—and close hard—and

Commend yourself if you're a
     salesperson.
Pat yourself on the back. Do you
     know why?
It is a tough racket. A lot of guys
     don't make it.
But how rewarding is it when you
     make that sale, when you shake
     their hand and close them?
It's a victory.
You're triumphant on the battlefield.
You've made the sale.
You've done the right thing for the
     client.
You're going to make a nice
     commission.

increase your sales. This is what I love. I eat and breathe closing. I love to close. I love when other people close.

Let me hear from you. Go out and make that sale, then send me an email. I have an 89-year-old mother and I still love to call her up when I make a big sale. She's thrilled to hear it and I'll be thrilled to hear about yours.

Get out there and close them. Remember, there's only one thing that counts—"Get them to sign on the line that is dotted."

I'm able to get that adjustment or sale
because I make the other guy feel
good. I'm going to close hard on this
case and really stay on him until I get
him. But I'm going to do it the right
way—the honest way. I'm going to get
into his head. I'm going to do a good
job for him. You do the same thing.

Epilogue

In closing, and I mean this literally and figuratively, it is imperative that you follow the techniques presented throughout this book word for word. We all must study and work to get what we want and need. And it is also important to remember everything comes from our Creator.

To be truly successful and "close the deal" in business and life, we can follow a higher road when making and breaking sales records. We can act honestly, fairly, and do the best for our clients, family, and community—not only ourselves. We can give some of our earnings to charity—with joy and without the need for recognition. It's important to set an example for others in thought, speech, and deed. We can show humility and treat others with respect and kindness.

And most of all, we can remember to give thanks to our Creator for all of our blessings, and even hardships, for we grow and hopefully become better people because of them. Each of us has our own unique purpose to fulfill. May our business practices and successes help us all achieve our individual purposes so that we will "*ABC—Always Be Closing*" in all areas of our life.

To be truly successful and "close the deal" in business and life, we can follow a higher road when making and breaking sales records. We can act honestly, fairly, and do the best for our clients, family, and community— not only ourselves.

Appendix I

Winning Salesmanship Checklist

The Basics

- Know and believe in your product; study, learn, practice, role-play.
- Check your ego at the door; learn from everyone.
- Be positive; he who does not have a smile on his face should not own a shop. Ask your Creator for assistance.
- Act with integrity, sincerity, and dress for success.
- Know your customers. Look directly at them. Watch their body language. What are they thinking? Why do they want this product? What's in it for them?
- Stress that you will do your best for your customers.
- Treat everyone like they're Donald Trump.
- Remember your time is valuable—don't waste it.
- Go with your back against the wall; be willing to take abuse.
- Get your foot in the door.
- Establish common ground quickly and close, close, close.
- Ask for the order. Give buyers time alone for discussion.
- Preempt buyer's remorse with rapport-building questions, follow-up phone calls, and paperwork.

Appendix II

Winning Salesmanship Closes

The Meet and Greet

- May I step in?
- May I help you?
- How are you doing?
- Where are you from?
- Let me show you our product.
- People are people—don't be afraid of your customers.
- What's your customer thinking about?
- Why would he want to buy this product?
- What's really in it for him?

Winning Salesmanship Closes

Initiating the Close

- Are you ready to own and take delivery of this product?

- Are the figures agreeable?

- Let me ask you a question. Can I go ahead and get an application for you?

- May I have a cash deposit of $____?

- May I have a totally refundable check for a deposit?

- May I have the keys to your trade-in?

- May I have your signature on the application or paperwork?

- May I have your order?

- Would you like to purchase this product?

- Are you willing to purchase this product?

- Are you able to purchase this product?

- Would you like to move forward?

- Would you like to take delivery today?

- May I have your social security number?

- May I see your driver's license?

Initiating the Close Continued

- I need to get some papers from my car.

- I want to check on something for you.

- I'd like to work for you. I'd like to deliver this product to you. Give me a second.

- Let's take a look at this.

- Are you ready to buy?

- Are you ready to do business today?

- Are you satisfied with the product and the presentation?

- Are you ready to own and take delivery?

- Are you ready to sign today if the figures and numbers are agreeable?

- Are you ready to move forward with this contract if all of the numbers and everything work out okay?

- We may need your spouse's signature.

Establishing Trust

- If it goes through, you're ready to have the coverage that you really need to protect your family.

- Give me a deposit on this house, and I'm really going to fight for you.

- I'm really going to work hard for you to go back and make that deal.

- I'm here to do for you.

- I'm here to work for you.

- I'm here to make a deal for you.

- I'm here to get you the best product—house, car, insurance, computer, timeshare—whatever it is.

- I'm here for you.

- I'm here to do the best I can for you.

Handling Objections

- Oh, just to satisfy my curiosity, why is it that you want to speak to this person?

- By the way, that is interesting. Why do you want to go and do that?

- Based on that, if they say it is a go, why don't we go ahead and put the figures together now, and write this up.

- Oh, I like what you're saying. Sure, go ahead and think about it. In the meantime, let's get you on paper and let's start to get this written up. We can always talk to So-and-So on the phone. We can make a phone call.

- Oh, I appreciate that. That's great that you want to think about it, but before we finish up today, just to satisfy my curiosity, what is it that you would like to think about?

- Okay, no problem. I'm going to see another client today, but before I leave, I'm just curious; what is it that you want to think about?

- Oh, you aren't interested in a car? You just want to pick up a brochure for six months from now? Are you kidding me, with the way car and gas prices are going? They are going to be way up. Right now we have phenomenal deals.

- Oh, the real estate market is down? Are you kidding me? Come on, you are going to get the best possible price imaginable.

- You know, we had that situation, and what do you think we did about it?

Handling Objections Continued

- You know, Mr. Jones, what would you do if you owned this dealership, and they were giving you poor service and you had the opportunity to do something about it? Well, that's exactly what we did. And now, our service is better.

- I'll see if I can get you that, and once we get you that, of course we have a deal, is that correct?

- Let me make a phone call. Let me call home office. Let me do this or that, and I'll see if I can get you that, and once we get you that, of course we have a deal, is that correct?

- Will you take that in black?

- Yes, we can get it in black. Let's go ahead and get the paperwork going.

Preempting Buyer's Remorse

Building Rapport After the Close

- Where do your kids live?
- Where did your kids grow up?
- Where's your family?
- Where are you from?
- Where did you go to school?
- What kind of work do you do?
- How did you become successful?
- Oh, you did this?
- You did that business? Wow—that must have been exciting!

Solidifying the Sale the Following Day

- I need additional signatures.
- I just checked with So-and-So and everything is going well.

Notes

1   Chapter 1-10 titles: quotes from *Glengarry Glen Ross*. James Foley, Director.. Film based on play by David Mamet. New Line Cinema, 1992.
2   YouTube: Founded in February 2005, YouTube is the leader in online video, a location to view and share original videos worldwide through a Web experience. Viewers can upload and share video clips on www.youtube.com.
3   Schmooze: Yiddish for chat; network; to talk in a friendly and persuasive manner, especially so as to gain favor, business, or connections.
4   Buyer's Remorse: Regret and doubt a buyer experiences after making a purchase, often of expensive items, creating uncertainty about keeping the purchase.
5   Schwartz, David J Ph. D. *The Magic of Thinking Big*, 131.
6   Schlepp: Yiddish for carry, lug, drag.
7   Ben Franklin Close, or Balance Sheet Close: The client is asked to make a list of positive and negative qualities of a purchase. Usually the list of negatives will be shorter, increasing the likelihood of the sale.
8   Tire Kicker: Someone who has no intention of buying, thereby wasting the time of a salesperson.
9   Lot Lizard: Prostitute who works at truck stops; someone not interested in buying.
10 Brick overcoat: Protective shield or defense used by someone, such as a buyer, to prevent them from succumbing to an unwanted or unfavorable situation.
11 Smoke Screens: Cover-ups, disguises.
12 Space Invaders: Arcade video game designed by Tomohiro Nishikado in 1978.

References

Boiler Room. Ben Younger, Director. Film. New Line Cinema, 2000.

Bristol, Claude M. *The Magic of Believing*. New York, NY: Simon & Schuster, 1969.

Carnegie, Dale. *How to Win Friends and Influence People*. New York, NY: Simon & Schuster, 1981.

Carnegie, Dale. *How to Stop Worrying and Start Living*. New York, NY: Simon & Schuster, 1984.

Chandler, Steve. *100 Ways to Motivate Yourself*. Franklin Lakes, NJ: Career Press, 2004.

Chandler, Steve and Sam Beckford. *100 Ways to Create Wealth*. Bandon, OR: Robert D. Reed Publishers, 2007.

Gay III, Ben. *The Closers*. Hampton House Publishing Company, Inc., 1988.

Girard, Joe and Stanley H. Brown. *How to Sell Anything to Anybody*. New York, NY: Simon & Schuster, 2001.

Glengarry Glen Ross. James Foley, Director. Film based on play by David Mamet. New Line Cinema, 1992.

Hopkins, Tom. *How to Master the Art of Selling*. New York, NY: Warner Books Edition, 1982.

Mukoff, Moshe, S.C. Mizrahi, Rebbe Nachman,and Breslov Research Institute. *The Gentle Weapon: Prayers for Everyday and Not-so-Everyday Moments: Timeless Wisdom from Rebbe Nachman* of Breslov. Woodstock, VT: Jewish Lights Publishing, 1999.

Pretty Woman. Garry Marshall, Director. Film. Touchstone Pictures, 1990.

Schwartz, David J Ph. D. *The Magic of Thinking Big*. New York, NY: Fireside Edition, Simon & Schuster, Inc. 1987.

Wall Street. Oliver Stone, Director. Film. 20th Century Fox, 1987.

Trump, Donald J. *The Art of the Deal*. New York, NY: Random House, 1989.

Ziglar, Zig. Selling 101: *What Every Successful Sales Professional Needs to Know*. Nashville, TN: Thomas Nelson, Inc., 2003.

About the Author

Larry Krakow, Boca Raton businessman,dedicated soldier of the Israeli Defense Force, and author, is always trying to make a difference. In the 1970s, his personal mission was to protect Israel and her people. Now, he is searching for ways to help people excel in business. With over twenty years of experience in the sales and marketing arena, he has been successful in all areas of salesmanship, and has been a top salesman in the country. "Closing" sales with integrity, finesse, and confidence, and helping others are two of his passions.

As a young American, Larry left the United States to fight for Israel. Proving to be a tough leader and soldier, he was rewarded with the honor to become a member of the elite Golani Brigade. Since the days he spent serving his homeland, Larry has lived a successful life and has been truly blessed.

An accomplished salesman, Larry will tailor techniques and closes precisely for you and your organization. Corporations, businesses, and independent salespeople will benefit from Larry's expertise, savvy and skill. If you're a business owner and have agents or sales people who report to you, he will suggest specific ideas and objectives for your team to close more effectively and more often. You can view this information on his website, www.winningsalesmanship.com.

Currently living in Delray Beach, Florida with his family, Larry practices "winning salesmanship" throughout South Florida, and devotes a portion of his attention to community activities.

Larry Krakow is grateful to have the opportunity to help his community and other business people prosper. Let his knowledge and experiences of "winning salesmanship" lead you to victory on the battlefield of business and in life.

ROBERT D. REED PUBLISHERS ORDER FORM

__Call in your order for fast service and quantity discounts__

(541) 347-9882

Fax: (541) 347-9883

__OR__ order on-line at **www.rdrpublishers.com** *using PayPal.*

__OR__ order by mail: Make a copy of this form; enclose payment information:

Robert D. Reed Publishers

1380 Face Rock Drive, Bandon, OR 97411

Note: Shipping is $3.50 1st book + $1 for each additional book.

Send indicated books to:

Name _____

Address _____

City _____ State _____ Zip _____

Phone _____ Fax_____ Cell _____

E-Mail _____

Payment by check /__/ or credit card /__/ *(All major credit cards are accepted.)*

Name on card _____

Card Number _____

Exp. Date _____ Last 3-Digit number on back of card _____

	Qty.
Winning Salesmanship—The Glengarry Way by Larry Krakow $11.95	_____
The Joy of Selling by Steve Chandler. $11.95	_____
100 Ways to Create Wealth by Steve Chandler & Sam Beckford $24.95	_____
Customer Astonishment by Darby Checketts $14.95	_____
The Chic Entreprenuer by Elizabeth Gordon. $12.95	_____
The Media Savvy Leader by David Henderson. $19.95	_____
How Bad Do You Really Want It? by Tom Massey. $19.95	_____

Other book title(s) from www.rdrpublishers.com:

_____ $ _____

_____ $ _____